EXPLORING WORLD CULTURES

Bolivia

By Rebecca Carey Rohan

Cavendish
Square

New York

Published in 2022 by Cavendish Square Publishing, LLC
243 5th Avenue, Suite 136, New York, NY 10016

Website: cavendishsq.com

This publication represents the opinions and views of the author based on his or her personal experience, knowledge, and research. The information in this book serves as a general guide only. The author and publisher have used their best efforts in preparing this book and disclaim liability rising directly or indirectly from the use and application of this book.

All websites were available and accurate when this book was sent to press.

Library of Congress Cataloging-in-Publication Data

Names: Rohan, Rebecca Carey, 1967- author.
Title: Bolivia / Rebecca Carey Rohan.
Description: First Edition. | New York : Cavendish Square Publishing, 2022.
| Series: Exploring world cultures | Includes index.
Identifiers: LCCN 2020037207 | ISBN 9781502658920 (Library Binding) | ISBN
9781502658906 (Paperback) | ISBN 9781502658913 (Set) | ISBN
9781502658937 (eBook)
Subjects: LCSH: Bolivia--Juvenile literature. | Bolivia--Description and
travel. | Bolivia--History--Juvenile literature. | Bolivia--Social life
and customs.
Classification: LCC F3308.5 .R65 2022 | DDC 984--dc23
LC record available at https://lccn.loc.gov/2020037207

Editor: Katie Kawa
Copy Editor: Nicole Horning
Designer: Jessica Nevins

The photographs in this book are used by permission and through the courtesy of: Cover cristianl/E+/Getty Images; p. 4 Encyclopaedia Britannica/Universal Images Group via Getty Images; p. 5 Jesus Merida/SOPA Images/LightRocket via Getty Images; p. 6 Anna Serdyuk/Moment Editorial/Getty Images; p. 7 hadynyah/E+/Getty Images; p. 8 Atlantide Phototravel/Corbis Documentary/Getty Images; p. 9 Bettmann/Getty Images; p. 10 JOSE LUIS RODRIGUEZ/AFP via Getty Images; p. 11 John Elk/The Image Bank/Getty Images; pp. 12, 25 AIZAR RALDES/AFP via Getty Images; p. 13 Tim Clayton/Corbis via Getty Images; pp. 14, 20 Apexphotos/Moment/Getty Images; p. 15 Anders Ryman/Corbis Documentary/Getty Images; pp. 16, 19, 24 Insights/Universal Images Group via Getty Images; p. 17 James Strachan/Photodisc/Getty Images; p. 18 Bim/E+/Getty Images; p. 21 Jose Luiz Quintana/LatinContent via Getty Images; p. 22 FotografiaBasica/iStock Unreleased/Getty Images; pp. 23, 27 Anders Ryman/The Image Bank Unreleased/Getty Images; p. 26 LUIS ACOSTA/AFP via Getty Images; p. 28 ICHAUVEL/Moment/Getty Images; p. 29 Thomas Janisch/Moment/Getty Images.

Some of the images in this book illustrate individuals who are models. The depictions do not imply actual situations or events.

CPSIA compliance information: Batch #CS22CSQ: For further information contact Cavendish Square Publishing LLC, New York, New York, at 1-877-980-4450.

Printed in the United States of America

Find us on

Contents

Bolivia is the fifth-largest country in South America. It's about the size of the U.S. states of California and Texas put together.

A journey across Bolivia would include many different

This map shows where Bolivia is. It also shows La Paz, which is the city at the center of Bolivia's government.

landscapes. The highest part of the country is in the Andes Mountains. The lowest part of the country is close to sea level, but the country itself doesn't border any oceans. Bolivia is a country of **extremes**—from plains to rain forests and from hot summers to snowy winters.

The people of Bolivia—also known as Bolivians—are as different as the lands around them. They have their own backgrounds, beliefs, and cultures, or ways of life.

These people are holding Bolivia's flag as they protest the country's government, calling attention to things they think need changing.

Bolivians have faced hard times. They haven't always had a good government. However, they still try their best to find ways to be happy and have fun. They enjoy sports and games. They spend time with family and friends, and they eat good foods. Let's learn more about life in Bolivia!

Bolivia covers 424,165 square miles (1,098,582 square kilometers). It's a landlocked country, which means it doesn't touch any oceans. Instead, it's surrounded by other countries: Argentina

Bolivia's Uyuni Salt Flats (Salar de Uyuni) are the world's largest salt flats. Salt flats are areas of land covered with salt.

to the south, Chile and Peru to the west, Brazil to the north and east, and Paraguay to the southeast.

The Andes Mountains run through Bolivia's western area in two ranges called the Cordillera

FACT!

The Amazon River system flows through Bolivia. The Amazon is the longest river in South America!

Lake Titicaca

Lake Titicaca, in northern Bolivia, is the world's highest commercially navigable lake. This means that boats and ships used for business can sail on it.

Occidental and the Cordillera Oriental. Between the two ranges is a high plain called the Altiplano. Valley regions, or areas, called the Yungas

A view of part of the Altiplano is shown here. This region is home to much of Bolivia's population.

and the Valles have many beautiful plants.

The lowlands of Bolivia are mostly rain forests and grasslands. This region makes up a large area of northern and eastern Bolivia, but it has a smaller population than other regions.

People have called what's now Bolivia home for thousands of years. A group called the Tiwanaku (or Tiahuanaco) set up an empire near Lake Titicaca that lasted

Parts of a Tiwanaku settlement can still be seen in Bolivia at the Tiwanaku **archaeological site**.

until the 1000s CE. In the 1400s, the Incas came from Peru and took over the area.

In the 1500s, Spain took over. The Spanish brought their own culture, the Spanish language,

The Spanish discovered silver in Bolivia's mountains and enslaved many native people to mine it. Enslaved Africans were also brought to Bolivia to do this hard and unsafe work.

In the late 1800s, Bolivia fought the War of the Pacific against Chile. Bolivia lost the war and also its coastland. This is how Bolivia became landlocked.

and the Roman Catholic religion, or belief system, to the area that would become Bolivia.

In 1809, Bolivians began fighting for their freedom from Spanish rule.

Shown here is a painting of Simón Bolívar, who helped end Spanish rule in many parts of South America.

Bolivia officially declared independence on August 6, 1825. The new country was named after the general Simón Bolívar, who helped free Bolivia from Spanish control.

Government

Bolivia's government has faced many periods of uncertainty. For many years after independence, it was ruled by **dictators**. Today, Bolivia has a president. The president is elected by Bolivians every five years.

Protests were held throughout Bolivia after the presidential elections of 2019.

In 2019, many Bolivians protested the reelection of President Evo Morales. In fact, Morales was forced to step down. In 2020, Luis Arce was elected president.

FACT!

Bolivia has had many constitutions throughout its history. A constitution is a document that sets up how a country is run and spells out the laws of the land.

The Capital Cities

Bolivia has two capital cities: La Paz and Sucre. La Paz is known as the administrative capital, which means the president lives there and the legislature meets there. Sucre is the capital according to the constitution, and the Supreme Court still meets there.

Bolivia's legislature, or lawmaking body, has a Chamber of Deputies with 130 members and a Chamber of Senators with 36 members.

Shown here is the building where Bolivia's Supreme Court meets in Sucre.

Like the United States, Bolivia has a Supreme Court. It also has a Constitutional Court that decides if laws follow the constitution.

Bolivia is rich in **natural resources**, but it's one of South America's poorest countries. Tin was once the most important part of its economy—its system of making, buying,

Mining has been a part of life in Bolivia for hundreds of years.

and selling goods. When tin prices dropped in the 1980s, other valuable **minerals** were mined and sold. These include copper, gold, lead, and zinc. In recent years, oil and natural gas have become important parts of Bolivia's economy.

Bolivia's basic unit of currency, or money, is the boliviano.

Time to Trade

Bolivia imports, or brings in, the most goods from China. Brazil and Argentina are also popular trading partners for Bolivia.

Bolivian farms produce crops that include soybeans, rice, sugarcane, Brazil nuts, and quinoa. Bolivian wines, produced near Tarija, are gaining attention around the world.

Quinoa has become an important crop in Bolivia. This seed is eaten like a grain and has become popular in countries such as the United States.

Many tourists, or visitors, come to Bolivia to enjoy its archaeological sites. Tourism is part of the service industry, or business. In Bolivia, almost half of the people who have jobs have service jobs.

The Environment

Bolivia is home to mountains, rain forests, valleys, rivers, and lakes. The environment, or natural world, in Bolivia is beautiful.

Shown here are llamas and flamingos in Bolivia.

Animals found in Bolivia include jaguars, spectacled bears, snakes, monkeys, and sloths. Andean condors—the largest flying birds in South America—share the Bolivian sky with toucans. Bolivian river dolphins, also called pink dolphins,

FACT!

Puya raimondii is a very tall plant in Bolivia. It can be 30 feet (9 meters) tall, and it flowers only once every 80 to 150 years

A Disappearing Lake

By 2015, Lake Poopó, which was one of the largest lakes in Bolivia, had dried up! Scientists believe global warming and the use of water for mining and farming made it dry up.

are found in this country too. Llamas are native to Bolivia, and so are alpacas, which provide long, soft wool. The vicuña is a wild **relative** of both and lives on the Altiplano.

This was once part of Lake Poopó, but there's no water left.

Many of these animals are in danger of losing their homes because people are cutting down trees in Bolivia. In addition, pollution has made some of the water in Bolivia unsafe for people and animals to drink.

About 11 million people live in Bolivia. Many Bolivians can trace their family history back to indigenous, or native, groups. The largest native groups are the Quechua and Aymara.

Shown here are Bolivian women wearing traditional outfits, including *aguayos*.

About one-third of the population are mestizos, or people of mixed native and European **descent**. White people, mainly of European descent, make up a small percentage of the population. Black people in Bolivia can often

FACT!

Evo Morales was Bolivia's first indigenous leader. He was born in an Aymara village.

Hats as Symbols

In the late 1800s, many Aymara women wore bowler hats from Great Britain. Now, younger people are bringing back these hats to show their pride in their culture.

trace their roots back to the enslaved people brought to this land by the Spanish.

Many Bolivians wear clothes that look like modern American outfits, such as jeans and simple dresses.

Bolivians have found ways to reconnect with their history. This includes the hats they wear.

However, some Bolivians—especially members of native groups—have been known to wear **traditional** clothing. Women sometimes wear long *pollera* skirts and *aguayos*, which are special cloths for carrying things.

Bolivia's native people used to live in rural, or country, areas. Some Bolivians still live in these areas, but most now live in cities and towns. Most people use buses and taxis to get around.

Cities such as La Paz have many houses and apartment buildings.

In the rural areas, homes are often made of adobe, which is a kind of brick made of sun-dried mud and straw. Children walk or ride their bikes to get to school.

FACT!

Many children, especially girls, in rural Bolivia don't finish school.

Income Inequality

A big problem in Bolivia is income inequality. This means that there's a big gap between how much money the richest people make and how much other Bolivians make. A small group of Bolivians hold most of the country's wealth.

Families make up an important part of Bolivian society. The father is considered the head of the household. Children can go to work to help their family from a young age. Grandparents sometimes live with their children and grandchildren.

Groups around the world are working to make education and health care better for Bolivians living in rural areas.

Religion

Most Bolivians are Roman Catholic. This is a branch of the Christian religion, which follows the teachings of Jesus Christ. The Roman Catholic religion was brought to

Shown here is the inside of one of Bolivia's many Catholic churches.

Bolivia by the Spanish in the 1500s. Catholicism was once the official religion of the country. In 2009, the new constitution said that the country would no longer have an official religion.

FACT!

In July 2015, Pope Francis— the leader of the Roman Catholic Church— visited Bolivia. He's from Argentina, Bolivia's neighbor.

Mother Earth

Pachamama, or Mother Earth, is a goddess honored by many indigenous Bolivians. She's thought to help the crops grow. Bolivians hold festivals, or gatherings, to honor her.

Today, Bolivians also follow other religions, including other branches of Christianity such as the Protestant religion. Other Bolivians still follow the beliefs of the native peoples

Bolivians often wear traditional clothes and take part in traditional dances to honor Pachamama.

who came before them. These include a belief in many gods and goddesses. These indigenous beliefs have sometimes mixed with Catholic practices to create religious traditions that are unique, or special, to Bolivia.

Language

Bolivia once had three official languages: Aymara, Quechua, and Spanish. Aymara and Quechua are native languages, and Spanish was brought to Bolivia in the 1500s, along with the

This sign, which is in Spanish, tells Bolivians and visitors where to find a public bathroom.

Roman Catholic religion. Today, Spanish and all indigenous languages are recognized as official in Bolivia. That includes more than 36 languages!

FACT!

Only a small percentage of Bolivians know a foreign, or outside, language, such as English.

Spanish is the language of the government. It's used in many Bolivian schools. Most Bolivians can speak and understand Spanish, even if they're more

Many Bolivian kids practice their Spanish at school.

comfortable speaking an indigenous language.

Bolivian Spanish sounds a little different from the kinds of Spanish spoken in other places. Also, speakers in different parts of Bolivia might sound different from one another.

The Eyes Have It

Looking people in the eye is important in Bolivia. In fact, people who don't keep direct eye contact when speaking with others may appear untrustworthy.

Arts and Festivals

Bolivia's artistic history has both Spanish and indigenous roots. The country's beautiful Roman Catholic churches and religious artwork show Spain's **influence**. Bolivian **folk art** can be traced back to early indigenous peoples.

Bolivian weavers make beautiful things to sell in markets.

Bolivian weavers are known around the world for their beautiful work. Blankets and other woven goods are popular items for tourists to buy. Many musical instruments are still made by hand in this country. Bolivian jewelry is very popular too.

Bolivia celebrates its independence from Spain on August 6.

A Hidden Tradition

Imagine starting a new year with new underwear! In Bolivia, it's a New Year's Eve tradition to wear a new pair of underwear in a certain color. For example, red will bring love, and yellow will bring money.

The Bolivian people celebrate, or honor, national holidays, and each region has its own local celebrations too. Carnaval (sometimes spelled Carnival) is one of Bolivia's biggest celebrations. It

Bolivia's most famous Carnival celebrations take place every year in the city of Oruro.

has music, dancing, and parades. It happens just before Lent, which is a time of prayer leading up to Easter.

Fun and Play

Bolivians like to watch and play sports, especially soccer. This sport is called football in Bolivia and many other parts of the world outside of the United States. Bolivians play football on the streets or in

Shown here are members of La Verde, which means "The Green" in English.

the fields. Bolivia has a national team, which is called La Verde. Most Bolivian cities also have their own football clubs.

FACT!

Bolivian soccer players are used to playing in the thinner air of the mountains and the Altiplano. Players from other countries might find it harder to breathe!

26

Bolivians enjoy other sports, too, including volleyball, basketball, and golf. Many Bolivians ride bikes, and car racing is also popular.

Bolivians can go to internet cafés to use computers if they don't have one at home.

Bolivians like to listen to the radio and watch TV. They also use the internet for fun and for work.

Getting Their News

Bolivians believe in a free press. Although many people go online to get their news, Bolivia still has many daily newspapers. Most major cities in Bolivia have their own paper.

Food

It's believed that potatoes were first grown in the Andes, so it makes sense that potatoes are popular parts of Bolivian meals. *Sopa de mani* is a traditional Bolivian

Bolivian farmers grow a lot of potatoes!

soup made with meat, vegetables, and peanuts. Potatoes play a big part in this dish!

Other kinds of fresh fruits and vegetables are grown in the lower regions of Bolivia. Grains such as quinoa are used in stews in the highlands.

FACT!

Bolivia is one of the few places in the world that doesn't have a McDonald's as of 2020.

The city of Sucre is the "chocolate capital" of Bolivia. It's where the country's most popular chocolate shops are found.

A popular morning snack is a *salteña*. It's a handheld pie stuffed with meat, potatoes, and other vegetables. *Api morado* is a tasty Bolivian breakfast drink. It's made from mashed purple corn, hot water, sugar, and cinnamon.

Shown here is a popular Bolivian breakfast: *api morado* and *pastel de queso*, which is a cheese-filled pastry.

Lunch is the main meal of the day in Bolivia. Bolivians eat dinner, too, but lunch is often much bigger.

Glossary

archaeological site	A place people can visit to see things left behind by a past society.
descent	The background of a person in terms of their family or nationality.
dictator	A person who rules a country with total power and often in a harmful way.
extreme	Something as far as possible from a middle ground or its opposite.
folk art	A kind of art made by common people that is often connected to community life and is passed down over many years.
influence	An effect one thing has on another.
mineral	Something that is formed naturally under the ground.
natural resource	Something that is found in nature that is valuable to humans.
relative	Something that belongs to the same family or group as something else.
traditional	Following what's been done for a long time.

Find Out More

Books

Nelson, Kristen Rajczak. *Ancient Inca Culture*.
New York, NY: PowerKids Press, 2017.

Owings, Lisa. *Bolivia*. Minnetonka, MN: Bellwether
Media, 2015.

Website

National Geographic Kids: Bolivia

*kids.nationalgeographic.com/explore/countries/
bolivia/*

Visitors to this website will learn fun facts
about Bolivia.

Video

Bolivia Vacation Travel Guide

www.youtube.com/watch?v=4ZxgBQA7cuY

This video gives travelers all the facts they'll need to
plan their own trip to Bolivia.

Index

About the Author

Rebecca Carey Rohan is the author of several books for children. She has written about everything from musicians and writers to scientists and birds. She loves to travel and learn about new places. Currently, she lives in Savannah, Georgia.